A Course in

Self-

Care

Heal Your Body, Mind & Soul
Through Self-Love and Mindfulness

Ankita S.

Contents

Introduction

Self-care is an act of self-love. It's a way of telling yourself that YOU matter – that your needs, wants and desires are important enough to be *joyously* met. The word 'joyously' is very important here as we often forget that taking care of our own self is truly a celebration of our existence.

In the true sense of the word, self-care isn't about just five or maybe twenty minutes of 'Me-time' every day. It's about creating a life in which you relish every moment of your existence. Real self-care is self-transformation in its highest form. It takes you to the realization that you are the creator of your own destiny and that you can have everything you want if only you allow yourself to believe so and work towards it.

Real self-care brings you in touch with who you truly are – your dreams, your hopes, your desires, and everything else that contributes to your definition of 'I' and mine. It helps you create a life of abundance and joy so that you never need a vacation from living that life.

This course will compel you to get in touch with your Truth. It might not be entirely comfortable at first but I urge you to persist no matter what. An amazing life isn't built by living within one's comfort zone.

I want you to push yourself to your limits and fall completely in love with yourself every day from now onwards. Creating the life of your dreams is the highest form of self-care. Of course, the exclusive 'Me-time' every day is the cherry on the cake that makes the process even more delightful.

Every human being is a complex organism physiologically, psychologically and emotionally. At the spiritual level, we are all made of the same fabric but the way our identities manifest in the material world is always unique. The problem with society is that it epitomizes one way of being as the only ideal everyone must aspire for.

For instance, at one point of time in history, women with rounded figures were held as the ultimate paragons of beauty. In our present times, being reed thin has become the norm and everyone is aspiring to look like an emaciated runway model.

Hence, in our society, it's considered radical when someone is brave enough to just be himself or herself. From now onwards, I want you to focus on who you really are. Instead of taking everything for granted and believing that you are this way or that way, I want you to get in the habit of questioning everything.

Surely, this is not going to be comfortable at first but you must get comfortable with being uncomfortable. After all, we come face-to-face with our real potential only after stepping outside the comfort zone.

I want you to find your own definition of success and become very successful. Just remember that real success is what happens within you and not necessarily outside of you. Who you become in the process of acquiring everything you have aspired for is far more important than the material wealth you have managed to amass.

I want to also remind you that health is the greatest wealth and peace of mind is the most precious asset (the only one worth guarding with all your might and at all costs). Success doesn't necessarily mean doing more – it means being at peace with who you are, where you have come from and where you are going. Real freedom doesn't come from having more but from wanting less. You don't become rich by hoarding more objects and money but from how richly you live your life while using with gratitude that which you do own. Being rich is about being content and real contentment doesn't come from wanting more but from giving more.

What Self-Care is Not?

We live in a strange world. While it's considered perfectly 'natural' to complain about life and walk around looking like a martyr, it's usually not seen in good light when a person proclaims that he loves himself or herself. Such a person is immediately termed a narcissist and made to feel guilty about how he or she feels.

In my opinion, the glorified self-effacement that is done in the name of humility is far more dangerous as it not only damages our self-esteem but also leaves us seeking approval and acknowledgement from others.

Narcissism versus Self-Love

There is a clear distinction between narcissism and self-love. A narcissist is someone who is obsessed with himself to the point that he thinks he is superior to anyone else. He doesn't mind going to any extent to prove this fallacy as truth.

On the other hand, someone with a tremendous amount of self-love possesses a very healthy sense of Self. She loves and accepts herself unconditionally without making comparisons with others. She is well aware of her flaws and is constantly working to be the best version of herself without any sense of self-loathing or guilt.

Hence, the primary difference between a narcissist and a self-loving person is the motivation they are driven by. The narcissist lives from a place of fear and ego because he has to constantly strive to look and appear better than everyone else. He cares a great deal about how others perceive him as he must command the adulation of others. A self-loving person, on the other hand, lives from a place of unconditional love and non-judgmental acceptance. She is not influenced by how other people see her as her sense of self is inherently very strong. There is nothing to prove to anyone or any unnecessary interest in how other people perceive her.

While it might look like the narcissist has a lot of self-confidence that is generally not the case. What he is showing to the world is usually just a facade of false ego. Anyone who is guided purely by love will never compare himself with another person. The narcissist is rather too preoccupied with proving how he compares and fares better in comparison with others.

Self-love, on the other hand, is guided by self-reliance. You learn to rely on yourself for meeting your need for approval, acceptance and appreciation. Hence, self-love goes hand-in-hand with self-acceptance. You have to accept yourself unconditionally in order to have real self-love.

It's important to remember that your relationship with yourself is the most important relationship for you in the whole world. Every other relationship is merely a reflection of this one relationship. Believe it or not, this is the truth. If you delve deep into this relationship, you will develop the insight to understand every other relationship in your life.

For example, if you feel that others don't accept you for who you are, then, you must analyze if you fully accept your own self unconditionally and without judgment. If you feel that others are critical of you, then, you must do some soul-searching to find out how critical you are of yourself.

People will always perceive you the way you perceive your own self, and I am not talking about what you believe to be true at the conscious level. Your behavior and your reactions are shaped by the impressions registered in the subconscious mind.

Self-Care Begins with Self-Acceptance

Self-care begins with self-acceptance. Just like you cannot love someone else unconditionally without first accepting them completely and without judgment, the same is true for you.

If the aircraft was about to crash, you will put on your own oxygen mask first, and only then help others, you must always look after yourself first. By taking good care of yourself, you build the ability to derive strength, nourishment, and sustenance from your own soul. You don't need another person to make you feel better about yourself because you are already feeling amazing.

This way you are able to have deeper and more meaningful relationships with others as you no longer enter relationships from a place of need. All your relationships become based on the desire to give unconditionally and wholeheartedly. When the other person does something good for you, you feel ecstatic because you were not expecting anything. Letting go of all expectations is the best thing you can do to experience great joy and gratitude in your relationships.

It's not too far-fetched to say that taking excellent care of yourself and loving yourself unconditionally is the pre-requisite for having deep meaningful relationships with others.

Never forget that you cannot pour from an empty cup.

What Self-Care is Not

So let's first dismiss all the wrong ideas people have about self-care.

SELF-CARE IS NOT:

➤ Selfishness
➤ Self-absorption
➤ Narcissism
➤ Egotism
➤ Egocentrism
➤ Ostentation
➤ Superiority complex

➤ Being Vainglorious

Now, the question is what to do if someone else tells you that you are any of the above just because you love yourself and like taking care of yourself?

The answer lies in understanding other people. You must ascertain the fact that most people don't like themselves, and they find it very hard to understand how anyone else can be so happy with their own self.

There is also a lot of guilt and shame associated with feeling good about oneself. These negative emotions are so deeply imprinted in people's psyche that they try to put down anyone who manages to break out of this cycle of shame of guilt. This doesn't mean that they are bad people who are consciously trying to put others down. They are most likely doing this unconsciously (at least, in most cases) behind the smokescreen of good intentions. Most people are too badly trapped by the mental conditioning they have received from family, society and educational institutions. They find it difficult to understand that they are encaged in a dangerous cycle of self-loathing that often manifests as loathing towards others.

The right way to deal with someone like this is to treat them with empathy and compassion. For this, you have to be mindful of where they are coming from. A person who loves himself will never try to bring another person down. We don't see others the way they are, but we see a reflection of our own self in others.

Understand that whatever they are saying about you has nothing to do with you – it has everything to do with how they see their own self.

What is Self-Care?

As stated earlier self-care begins with self-acceptance. You must know who you truly are and accept yourself unconditionally. In fact, I don't even like to use the word 'accept' in this context. The right term would be 'embrace yourself unconditionally.' There are already enough critics in the world to bring people down. Why join their league and become your own worst enemy?

Where there is acceptance, love always follows. Love can never exist without acceptance preceding it first. In this book, you will take this journey with me from self-acceptance to self-love. Self-care comes automatically in the presence of these two.

If you do each assignment exactly as instructed, then, you certainly will succeed in creating a happier life for yourself. Self-care is so incredibly empowering that you will be amazed by all the transformations that will occur in your life.

Self-care is greatly emancipating because it makes you lose the desire or need to seek approval from others. You no longer get easily hurt by other people's words and actions. And even if you do feel hurt, you are able to respond back with calmness and composure.

Put Yourself First

Caring for yourself means taking out time for yourself every single day. It means understanding your needs and putting yourself first. After all, if you are second priority to your own self, then, everyone else in your life will also treat you that way.

SELF-CARE IS:

✓ Knowing the needs of your body, mind and soul

✓ Fulfilling your needs with joy and gratitude

✓ Honoring your desires and wants

✓ Taking out time for yourself without feeling guilty

✓ Exercising regularly and eating healthy

✓ Feeding positive ideas and thoughts into your mind

✓ Spending money on yourself without guilt

✓ Getting comfortable receiving compliments graciously and without undue self-effacement

✓ Saying a clear 'NO' to people, situations and places that suck your energy

✓ Spending time with those you love and/or who make you feel good about yourself

✓ Guarding yourself against negativity

✓ Not letting criticism or the negative words/opinions of others affect you

✓ Practicing compassion and forgiveness towards your own self (this will automatically make it easier for you to forgive others)

✓ Looking in the mirror and admiring everything you love about yourself

✓ Being grateful for everything you have and the person that you are

✓ Being kind to your body by listening to what it's telling you

✓ Constantly engaging in positive self-talk and encouragement

✓ Getting up and making a stronger comeback every single time you fall down

✓ Believing that you are the most important person in your world and treating yourself that way

✓ Doing whatever it takes to retain your happiness and positivity each day

The 10 Commandments of Self-Care

I recommend that you read these 10 commandments every day. You can paste them on your wall so that you are constantly reminded to practice them.

1. Love and accept yourself (unconditionally) first. Loving and accepting everyone else will come easily after this.

2. Take care of your body. This body is the only real home you have for living in this world.

3. Think positive, speak positive and listen only to what's positive.

4. Rely only on your own self. Believe that YOU have the power to make all your dreams come true. Do not seek approval from anyone else – believe in your own self no matter what anyone else says. If something feels right, then just trust your heart and go for it.

5. Make compliments a way of life. Give them generously to yourself and to others. If someone gives you a compliment, accept them graciously.

6. Treat yourself with dignity and respect. Walk away from everything that no longer serves your Highest Good.

7. Make your entire life a labor of love. Dream and create a life you don't need any days off from.

8. Every day, take the time to connect with Nature in some way. She is your mother entering her womb will take you closer to your own Truth

9. Compete only with your own self. Strive to constantly be a better than the best version of yourself.

10. Be completely honest with yourself – take responsibility for your life and for everything that you are experiencing right now.

Always Listen to Your Heart

I'll end this chapter with a little advice that you'd want to remember all throughout this course and also for the rest of your life. You'd want to hold on really tight to this piece of wisdom.

If you really want something, just go for it! Don't let anyone tell you it's not possible, it cannot be done, it's not practical. Life is what you make of it. Everything is a creation and if you are relying on someone else's idea of what's possible and what's not, then you are imposing their self-created limitations on your own life. Don't listen to anyone who says it can't be done. Learn to be your own best friends. Believe in your dreams and go after what you want.

How to Use This Book

This book is designed as a course meant to be taken over a period of three months. There are four lessons in each month that are meant to be studied and practiced every day of the week. If you want you can read the entire book in one go but to get maximum benefits out of this carefully designed course, I'd suggest taking things slow and following the step-by-step instructions.

You'll experience great transformation if you do all the exercises that are suggested for the week. I'll suggest starting out on a Sunday or a Monday so that it is easier for you to keep track of your progress. This isn't imperative – you can start on any day of the week – all you have to do is keep track of your progress properly.

It's very important that you are doing something for yourself every single day over a period of three months as you are establishing a habit here. At first, it might be very difficult for you to find time for yourself.

When you do something with consistency for a period of 21 days, it starts becoming a habit. Over time, self-care will become such a natural part of your routine that it will become as pivotal as brushing your teeth and taking a shower every day.

What if You Miss a Day?

In a perfect world, you will be reading and practicing the weekly lesson every day. However, things happen. Sometimes life just gets in the way and we feel like we have little control over our day.

My advice would be to avoid a situation like this as much as possible. Discipline is a pre-requisite for success in any area of life. If despite your best efforts, you end up missing a day, then, I would say get back to the schedule as soon as you can.

What you must watch out for is the trap of "I'll start tomorrow." This usually happens if you miss one day. Then, you will feel so guilty about having missed a day that you'd find it difficult to regain the momentum. This is the real danger with missing one day. It makes you lose your momentum and leaves you with guilt.

If you miss a day, then just accept it lovingly and try your best to not let it happen again. Don't beat yourself about it and don't allow yourself to feel guilty under any circumstance. Start from where you had left and you'd do great.

However, you must guard against making a habit out of this. Self-care is an empowering habit that you are building, and every day that you spend doing something good for yourself counts in helping you internalize it more deeply.

What if You Want to Skip a Lesson or an Activity

I would highly recommend that you practice every single lesson outlined in this course. A lot of times the mind will try talking us out of something that is difficult for us. You have to understand that this perception of difficulty usually stems from deep-seated mental blocks. If you practice each lesson for the entire week, then you will surely experience a shift – it might be a small or a big one but the shift will surely happen.

You might want to skip some activities – I would recommend that you try doing each activity at least for a few days if not for the entire week. This will help you understand whether it's something you can incorporate into your daily routine for the long-term or not. Ideally, practice each activity for at least a week.

Some activities will be especially enjoyable to you and those are the ones you'd want to adopt for life or for as long you wish to be practicing them.

How to Get the Most Out of This Book

➤ Read the weekly lesson every day of the week. Ideally, read it twice a day – right after waking up and immediately before going to bed.

➤ Maintain a daily journal in which you set goals for each day based on the instructions for the week.

➤ Feel free to take notes and make highlights in the book wherever necessary.

➤ Keep this book as a companion with you at all times. Some of you might find it helpful to own both a digital and paperback version of this book so that you can make highlights and take notes in the paperback version and use the digital version for a quick read throughout the day.

➤ Even though each lesson is meant to be studied for one week, you don't have to become perfect at it within such a timeframe. What's important is to make your best effort throughout the week and then continue the learning process for as long as it takes. You can progress to the next week's lesson while also continuing to master the previous week's lesson.

➤ For convenience, it might be better to read the first lesson of this book on a Sunday and start implementing it from Monday. This way, you'd know what to expect to be doing in the first week of the course. Starting on a Monday and ending the week on a Sunday will also help you in keeping track of your weekly progress.

➤ As you progress from week to week and lesson to lesson, you'd want to naturalize everything you are learning into a routine. Be sure to include those activities that you enjoy most in your daily or weekly routine.

➤ This is the kind of book that you'd want to keep coming back to time and again. The more number of times you go through the course, the greater will be your mastery over it. I recommend that once you finish the course, you restart it from lesson 1. Alternatively, you can choose to go through those lessons that you found especially enjoyable or those that were a challenge for you and where you feel you need to make considerable progress.

➤ If you have someone in your life who is on the same wavelength as you and that person would be interested in something like this, then, I would highly recommend doing the course with that person. Having an accountability buddy will help you make greater progress as you both will keep a check on each other's progress.

These are only some of the recommendations that I feel will be helpful to anyone who wants to get the most out of this book. However, you must experiment and see what works for you and what does not. Use your creative freedom to find your own way of getting the most out of this course.

To make a start somewhere, use the guidelines stated above. If something seems to work, then stick with it. If it doesn't, then find what works best for you and stay with it.

The Self-Care Course

Week 1 – Acknowledge and Accept Yourself

Self-care is all about self-love. Most of us find it very hard to love and accept our own self. I want you to understand that you can never truly love and accept another person without loving and accepting yourself first.

If you don't agree with this, then think about it again. Is there someone in your life whom you love immensely? How do you feel about them? Do you like everything about them or do you feel that they would be perfect if only some things would change. Most likely, you want to change some things about them even though you know that they will most likely never change (at least, not until they decide to change which is something you have very little control over).

Now, I want to ask you – do you love yourself unconditionally and accept who you are completely? I am not suggesting being smug and not having any aspiration to improve. Unconditional love and acceptance is all about being at peace with who you are at this very moment (with all your imperfections). You can change something only after you have accepted it completely. When you accept yourself with love and gratitude, you also allow yourself to become a better version of yourself.

Making yourself better by first accepting where you are in life right now is like teaching a baby how to walk. You won't scold and chide a baby when it is learning to walk. You'll cheer him on for every step he takes in the right direction. You'll celebrate the falls and the failed attempts alike as they are all part of the process of learning to walk. You must treat yourself the way you'd treat that beautiful baby.

If you don't love and accept yourself unconditionally, then the opinions of others will matter more to you than it should. You'll seek acknowledgment, acceptance and appreciation from others. This is a dangerous practice as you are allowing someone else to decide your worth while not fully comprehending that people don't see you the way you really are. Instead, everyone only sees a reflection of their own self in you.

Seek acknowledgment, acceptance, love and appreciation only from your own self. Become your own favorite person and bask in the glory of self-contentment. No, this is not going to turn you into a narcissist. Instead, it will make you a more compassionate person who is motivated by the desire to 'give' rather than by the desire to 'take.'

Real self-love makes you indestructible. It empowers you to face any challenge of life without requiring the crutch of outside motivation. Accepting your own greatness and uniqueness doesn't require making comparisons with others.

The sun doesn't compare itself with the moon, a rose doesn't compare itself with a marigold, a skylark doesn't compare itself with a nightingale. There is room enough for all of us to be amazing without stepping on each other's shoes.

Let the inner love flow towards your own heart. After that, you'll have ample compassion to offer to others. Your example will inspire others to love and accept their own self. You'll be a beacon of love and beauty in this world. Hence, be gentle and compassionate towards yourself. You are your own greatest responsibility.

Task for This Week:

Stand in front of a mirror and look into your own eyes. This might be hard but you must persist. Say to yourself, "I forgive you, I love you unconditionally, I accept you exactly the way you are." Do this exercise every morning and evening for at least 5 minutes. It's very important that you maintain eye contact with yourself in the mirror throughout this process. Repeat the sentences out aloud in the privacy of your room or bathroom. It doesn't have to be so loud that others can also hear it. Do what you feel most comfortable with. However, it's important to speak out the words as otherwise you'll mind will start wandering elsewhere.

If you are worried that accepting yourself the way you are will remove all motivation to change those qualities about yourself that you find undesirable, then let me assure you that's not what this practice does. In fact, you will find it much easier to bring about positive change in yourself once you start truly accepting yourself for the way you are right now. By accepting yourself for who you are in this moment, you are acknowledging yourself and giving love to yourself while appreciating the journey that you have taken to become the person that you are right now.

Once you have accepted yourself, you are no longer trying to swim against the tide or being unrealistic about your current reality. From this point on, it becomes easier to become the person that you truly want to be because now you know where you stand and from there you can move towards becoming your best self. Now, if you don't acknowledge where you are currently standing, then how can you take the road that leads to your best self?

Do this exercise at least twice a day every day (you can do it more number of times if you like but don't aim for any less than twice a day. I highly recommend doing this early in the morning – within 45 minutes of waking up – and at night, right before going to bed).

Week 2 – Deepen Your Relationship with Yourself

Which is the most important relationship in the world?

Whether you currently realize this or not – the most important relationship in the world is the one that you have with your own Self. How you relate with your own Self sets the ground for how others relate to you.

The outer world is only a mirror to your inner reality. The relationships you have with other people are, in some way, a reflection of the relationship you have with yourself.

We discussed the importance of self-acceptance last week. This week, let me ask you again:

Do you like yourself? Do you love yourself unconditionally? Do you see the good in yourself? Or do you constantly beat yourself up for the flaws that you think you possess?

I have said it before, and I'll say it again. Accepting and loving yourself unconditionally is the very foundation of a life of self-care.

Even if no one has said this to you yet – I am going to say this to you today, and you better start believing it! You are beautiful, you are amazing, you are gorgeous – you deserve the best that life has to offer. There never was, never has been, and never will be another one exactly like you in this world or in any other. You must reclaim your power and your gifts from the Universe by acknowledging the limitlessness of your soul and the inherent beauty of your individuality.

Get past the scarcity mindset by ceasing to compare yourself with others. You can only be the protagonist of your own story and your story is just as unique as you are. When you compare yourself with others you fail to realize that your only competition is with your own self. As long as you are striving to constantly grow and become a better person than who you were yesterday, you are living the true potential of your soul.

There is room enough for all of us to be gorgeous, amazing and superbly brilliant. Which flower ever craves to be like another one? Yet, each flower is so incredibly beautiful in its own unique way. If you go to any natural place, you will realize that nature is all about harmony and co-existence. The wind is not competing with the water. The sun is not competing with the moon. The forest is not competing with the desert.

Nature has so much variety, yet every element present in it is unique and beautiful in its own way. There is no competition. Human beings are also meant to be the same way. Each of us is a diamond shining with its own distinctive luster and brightness.

From now on, put a full stop on all comparisons, and start relishing your own individuality. There just can't be another you.

Never forget that the secret to stop comparing yourself with others is to love and accept yourself unconditionally. The more you are in love with yourself, the less chances there will be of you wanting to compare yourself with anyone else.

This week, I want you to be watchful of your internal talk with yourself – start noticing all the self-sabotaging thoughts/activities you indulge in. A life of self-care requires you to shed your true self in all its magnificent glory without being weighed down by any excess baggage.

We are usually very hard on ourselves. If only we could see ourselves from the eyes of those who love and admire us, it wouldn't be so difficult to accept our own inherent perfection.

No matter what you believe about yourself, trust me you are a far more amazing person than you think you are.

Tasks for This Week:

➤ Start paying attention to the voice inside your head – What does that voice say to you? Does it say things like: you're not good enough, you'll never get what you want, you'll always be a loser. Instead of suppressing or indulging in these thoughts, just observe them as they come and go.

➤ Keep a diary at hand (can be digital) and write down all the prominent self-sabotaging thoughts as they occur through the course of the day.

➤ Continue doing the mirror exercise twice a day. You'd ideally want to make this a permanent part of your life. If you aren't ready to do that, then continue for at least one more week. From now onwards, I want you to add another line to the existing one, "I forgive you, I love you unconditionally, I accept you the way you are. You are gorgeous, you are amazing, you are incredibly beautiful, you are perfect, I love you the way you are."

Week 3 – Spend Time with Yourself & Reward Yourself

How easy or hard has been for you to love and accept yourself unconditionally so far? If you are like most people, then this has likely not been an easy journey for you. You might be struggling with crippling self-doubt, constant self-abnegation, and instant self-criticism.

I just want to tell you that no matter where you are in your journey right now, things ARE GOING TO START LOOKING UP if you only persist with this course and continue doing what you must do to get to your goal of effortless self-care and boundless self-love.

Now, let me ask you something: What do you do when you are in love with someone?

You give them all your attention and spend as much time as you possibly can with them. Isn't it?

Have you been spending any time with yourself without constantly looking for distractions so that you don't have to face the voice within your own head? Today I want to urge you to spend time with yourself. Dare to be alone with no one but your own self for company. No matter how uncomfortable this makes you, I want you to do it and I want you to start from today. Also remember that growth starts at the end of our comfort zone. Greatness is not achieved by living a comfortable life – it is achieved by constantly moving out of our comfort zone to face new challenges that compel us to raise our standards and hold up our own self to a new much higher one.

What do you do when you are trying to build a relationship with someone? You spend time with them. Isn't it?

This week, I dare you to be alone – completely alone (even if it is only for 5 minutes). During this alone time, watch the thoughts that float in your mind, the memories that gain shape in the ether of your consciousness, the emotions that swell up within the depths of your heart. I dare you to experience it all without trying to run away from anything.

Watch your own consciousness unfold itself to you without judgment, and also without indulgence. Allow what is coming to come in its own accord, and let go when it must go.

Reward Yourself

This week, reward yourself for sticking to this self-care course so far. **If something gets rewarded, it is much more likely to be repeated.**

Even if you have not been consistent, appreciate yourself for all the efforts that you have made. From now on, make a commitment to be more consistent.

Consistency is far more important than perfection. Making some effort every single day to improve your life is much more fruitful than making a lot of effort once in a while. Make alterations to the practices if you are finding it impossible to fit them into your current schedule. For instance, if you are able to find the time to do the mirror exercise only in the afternoon, then, do it in the afternoon. Implementing what you are learning is more important than implementing everything with perfection. Slow and steady always wins the race!

If you still think you don't have time to do all the exercises, then I'll challenge you to keep track of your day and account for how you are spending your time. All of us have 24 hours in a day. It's how this time is utilized that determines whether one will be successful or not. If you are spending

10 minutes every day looking at social media, then that time can easily be utilized to do the mirror exercise.

Looking at other people's pictures on social media is not going to change your life but putting in the work to change your own self is certainly going to transform your reality. I challenge you to start today!

Even if you have been consistent the whole time, I would still urge you to look into your daily schedule and see how you can take things to the next level. Eliminate unproductive activities as much as you possibly can. You can always do better than you think you can do.

Lastly, **don't forget to reward yourself for every little progress that you do make.** I'll repeat myself again, *if something gets rewarded, it is much more likely to be repeated.* If your goal is to get in great shape and you haven't been able to make it to the gym, then break this goal down into smaller steps. Start with a run around the block. If even that seems too hard, then just go out for a walk. If even that seems hard, then simply get up from your seat and walk around the house.

You must reward yourself in some way by appreciating your efforts consistently. This week, give yourself a reward for all the things that you have done well so far. Resolve to make next week a better one. Note down your weaknesses and make a plan to overcome them in the coming weeks. It doesn't have to be an absolute plan that will lead you from 0 to 100 in a matter of 7 days but one that helps you make some improvement even if the improvement is only by a meager 0.0001%. If you retain consistency and keep charging ahead with momentum, one day you won't even realize it and you would have arrived at the highest peaks of success. Just keep charging ahead! There is no other success mantra that works better.

Tasks for This Week:

➤ Reward yourself by doing something you truly enjoy. It could be a relaxing bath, a delicious meal that you love, a day at the spa or just about anything that truly makes you feel joyful and pampered.

➤ Spend time alone with yourself this week. It could be just 5 minutes or an hour or as long as you can manage. Be with yourself without any distractions. Switch off your phone or keep it in a different room. Get off the internet and cut off all communication with others for this period. Take a walk alone or just lie down on your bed practicing deep breathing (but don't fall asleep).

➤ Witness all the thoughts, emotions, and memories that emerge within the landscape of your mind. Watch them without attachment or judgment. Remember that you are not your thoughts, your emotions, or your memories. You are the witness of everything that is happening in you, around you, and through you.

➤ You are the imperishable omnipresent consciousness. You are a drop in the ocean of infinity, and yet within that drop the entire infinity is contained. When you begin accepting yourself for whatever you maybe in this moment, you also develop the power to become who you truly want to be and make your life what you want it to be. It all starts with becoming an observer of your thoughts, memories and emotions without judgment, criticism or any desire to hold on to anything.

➤ Continue writing all the self-sabotaging thoughts that occur to you. Did these thoughts become even more forceful when you were alone? Be sure to note down those thoughts that recur with the highest frequency.

➤ Continue doing the mirror exercise every day if you have been enjoying it so far.

Week 4 – Celebrate Yourself

You become the person that you believe you are. If you believe you are smart and beautiful, that is what you will eventually become. If you believe you are a loser who can't do anything right, then that is the reality you will create for yourself. And by believing, I don't mean what you think of yourself or try to think of yourself in your conscious mind. I mean what you truly believe to be true for yourself within your subconscious mind.

The people around you simply mirror your own beliefs about yourself. You are constantly emitting thought vibrations about what you believe to be true for yourself. Any person who comes in contact with your aura picks up these vibrations and starts treating you the way you think you deserve to be treated.

Have you ever noticed how on those days when you look in the mirror and say, "I'm looking very good today," you end up receiving a lot of compliments. Then, there are those days when you look in the mirror and say, "I look awful. I'm a total mess." On that day, it seems like every other person is reaffirming this idea to you.

You might ask that how someone who is in an abusive relationship is asking to be treated that way. There can be a lot of possible explanations to this. You have to first understand that everything in life is a choice including staying in an abusive relationship. Some people might say that it's not a choice for them and it's something they 'have to' do irrespective of their desires.

I'll emphasize again, it's a choice – in this case a choice to not take a stand for themselves and face the consequences of walking out of the relationship. For some reason or another, a victim of abuse deeply believes that he or she 'has to' suffer and that there's no way out.

That person might be afraid to face the consequences of severing his or her relationship with the abuser. In that person's mind, the consequences of leaving the abusive relationship might be far worse than the consequences of bearing the abuse. It could also be that the victim grew up watching one parent abuse the other. As a result, the idea that abuse is an inherent part of an intimate relationship has become so deeply ingrained in that person's subconscious mind, that he or she is not even able to recognize this fact.

It's the same with any challenging situation in life. The life you are living right now is a reflection of your most deeply held beliefs. In order to transform your life from the inside out, you have to first change your ideas about life, and then train yourself to feel the right emotions that support your new belief system.

If thoughts are the cars that take you to your destination, then emotions are the fuel that runs the car in the first place. You must create the appropriate emotions to go with the right thoughts.

This isn't going to be easy but nothing worthwhile is ever easy. If you want to change your life, you have to work for it every day without any excuses and without giving up no matter how tough the going gets. However, this kind of work can also be a lot of fun.

This week you will do a special exercise. I would request you to go through the most frequently occurring self-sabotaging thoughts and write positive affirmations to replace them.

I would urge you to start training yourself to feel the emotions that match these positive affirmations. Of course, initially, when you start repeating a positive affirmation like, "I am wealthy, I am abundant, I am gorgeous, I am stunning," the little voice in the head will say to you, "You fool, you are broke, you are miserable, you are ugly, you are awful."

You have to learn to ignore that voice and persist despite everything it might say. Over time, this negative voice will become weaker as the new positive voice will get stronger. Don't expect this to happen overnight.

It might take a few weeks or even year but you'll get there eventually. Celebrate every little victory along the way. You will make massive progress by taking just a few steps in the right direction every day with consistency.

Try to carry your positive affirmations with you wherever you go. You might want to make a few copies so that you have at least one copy with you at any time of the day.

Throughout the day, stay observant of the thoughts that emerge in your mental landscape and the feelings that bubble up in your heart. Every time a negative thought comes up or a negative feeling begins to suck you in, quickly take action and start reading your positive affirmations. Read it out aloud if possible and make yourself feel as if what you are saying is really true. You must fake it till you make it!

Tasks for This Week:

➤ I want you to go through all the self-sabotaging thoughts you have written down. Find out if there is a common theme? Do they pertain more strongly to one area of your life than with others? For instance, are your limiting beliefs and personal sense of failure centered around the area of health or is it around money? Most likely, it will pertain to that area in which you are currently the weakest. I want you to replace each of the prominent self-sabotaging thoughts with a self-affirming one. For instance, if your self-sabotaging thought is, "I am ugly" replace it with "I am beautiful." Make a list of all the positive affirmations that are going to replace your self-sabotaging thoughts from now on.

➤ If you are still doing the mirror exercise, then include the affirmations in your routine. If you are not doing the mirror exercise any more (which I highly recommend doing), then you can do the affirmations as a standalone practice every morning and evening. Do them the same way you were doing the mirror exercise. It would be great if you can do it in front of a mirror but it's not mandatory.

➤ If possible, practice the affirmations at least twice a day. If not, then do it at least once a day. In addition, whenever you have any free time throughout the day, read your affirmations and feel as if what you are saying is already true for you. You don't need to read it out aloud every time. You can just read it in your mind if other people are around you. The most important thing is to feel as if every word is real and match your emotions with what you are saying.

➤ Every time a negative thought begins to form in your mind, quickly turn to your affirmations and start repeating them.

Week 5 - Eliminate Clutter and Create an Inspiring Space

Clutter not only affects the aesthetics of your outer environment but also the beauty of your inner space. Just try meditating in a room that has dirty laundry strewn around and you will know what I mean. It won't be too far-fetched to say that your environment is your mind. You just can't think clearly enough as long as you have untidiness surrounding you.

This week, I would like you to eliminate clutter from your life. Eventually, I want you to work on both your inner and your outer environment. To get started, we will focus on the outer clutter.

I'd suggest that you start identifying what is truly important to you. Begin the decluttering process by removing everything that you don't use anymore or that's broken and non-functional.

Donate the clothes that you no longer wear and let go of things you don't use anymore. If you haven't needed something for 2 years, then you are likely never going to need it.

If you take a look at your wardrobe, then you will realize that you regularly reach out only for a few pieces. I don't mean that you get rid of everything you don't regularly wear. I'm just suggesting that you surround yourself with clothes and things that you truly cherish so that every time you look at your possessions, you feel uplifted by their beauty.

I personally like Marie Kondo's method of holding each item in your hands and asking yourself if it sparks joy. Most of the time the answer is straight forward but sometimes it is not. Sometimes an item does not spark joy but it has sentiments attached to it. In such a case, it becomes very difficult to decide what to do with it. I would suggest that if something doesn't spar joy and yet you are not ready to part with it, then it might be better to use it in a way that would spark joy.

For instance, a sentimental coffee mug can become a pen holder for your table. Look for creative ideas to use these kind of items.

There are those items that don't spark joy but are essential for maintaining hygiene and health: for instance, the dust pan or the broom. Again, storing them in an aesthetically pleasing way (perhaps behind a charming closet door) would help.

Letting go of things that you feel attached to is one of the hardest things to do in life. It is almost like letting go of a friend's hand who is no longer alive. You feel guilty as it seems like there is something you can do for it. But once you gone through the process and managed to let go of everything that no longer serves your highest good, you feel exhilarated and light.

There is a lot more freedom in having fewer items that you truly cherish than in being weighed down by having too many possessions that don't spark any joy. Let go of excess baggage to travel light through life.

I would suggest that you start out by decluttering just one small area of your house this week. You can spend the first three days removing all the clutter from this area and making it as clean and organized as possible. It could be your work desk, your bedroom, your closet – any place from which eliminating clutter will really help you right now.

During the latter part of this week, I would like you to work on turning this space into an inspiring one. What can you add to this space to make it more inspiring – so much that it becomes a delight for you to look at?

This might mean hanging a beautiful chandelier in your closet or placing a flower vase on your work desk. It could also mean adding aromatic candles to your bathroom or placing storage baskets in your linen closet.

The point is that this space should feel inspiring and beautiful to you. You are the only one who knows exactly what you must do to make it happen.

For this, you'll have to find out what you like seeing, having, and experiencing in your environment the most.

Elimination is a very important part of the process as through elimination you make space for the new. However, inspiration is equally important as it invites into your life what you truly cherish and want more of.

Once you have mastered the art of eliminating clutter from a particular space and turning it into an inspiring one, I would suggest that you extend this practice to other spaces in your life.

Over time, this will likely become addictive as you would want to live in nothing less than a sanctuary of peace and beauty.

Tasks for This Week:

➤ Choose one space and remove thoroughly declutter it. Start small, so that you don't feel too overwhelmed by this task. It could be just your work desk or an armoire in your room. Once you have eliminated clutter make the space as clean and organized as possible. Be sure to have a place for everything and develop the habit of returning things to their designated space after each use. You can take up to three days to satisfactorily complete this task. Of course, you can take longer if that's what feels right to your heart but this is the timeline I would recommend.

➤ Once you have made the space clean and organized, it is time to make it more inspiring. Is there anything you can add to it that would make it a delight for you to behold every time? Spend the remaining four days turning that space into an inspiring one. Strive to make it a space so warm and uplifting that by being in or around it, you automatically feel cocooned in beauty.

➤ If successfully completing this project makes you feel good, then slowly transform your entire house and workspace into inspiring spaces.

Week 6 – Working with Inner Clutter

There is nothing more detrimental and damaging than a cluttered mind. Being unorganized with your life and impulsively attacking every task that comes up is a surefire way to make yourself miserable. You must apply the Pareto Principle here. According to this principle, 80 percent of your results come from 20 percent of the actions that you do. Therefore, in order to maximize your results, you must focus all your energy on this 20 percent that is going to bring you substantial returns on your efforts.

I'd suggest that you remove clutter from your inner landscape just the way you removed clutter from your outer space. Begin the process by first learning to manage your time.

I can't emphasize this enough but time is your greatest asset. How you manage this finite resource will determine how successful or not so successful you are in life. Therefore, I would like you to start by writing down how you are spending your time.

Keep a journal with you – it could be on your phone or in a handwritten diary – to account for every moment of your day. Write down exactly what you are doing hour-by-hour if not minute-by-minute. It might seem stressful at first but holding yourself accountable is the only way you can increase your efficiency.

I must warn you that this exercise might not be comfortable as a lot of times we don't want to fully accept how we are spending our time. It's also very easy to fall for the "I'll start tomorrow" trap when you think you'd be following your ideal schedule. This is almost like saying that a fat person will start exercising once they have gotten thin. You have to start now so that you can analyze your life exactly the way it is right now.

Getting to know where you currently are in your journey is the most important step that you can take towards becoming your best self. Spend at least 2-3 days tracking your time in this manner.

Thereafter, I want you to analyze the data you have collected. How much time did you spend talking on the phone, how much time did you spend being super productive at work, how much time did you spend watching TV, etc?

You must analyze the data with complete dispassion and detachment. This is very important otherwise you can easily fall for the guilt-trip which would lower your self-esteem and prevent you from taking the measures to completely change your life.

I want you to look at each of the activities you are regularly engaging in and determine how it's adding value to your life or if it's not adding any value to it. For this, I would suggest taking yourself back to the emotional state you were in while performing each activity.

For instance, did you feel good about yourself after you hung up the phone having gossiped with your friend for 1 hour? What kind of emotions did this activity leave you with? Did it make your life any better or did it feel like taking two steps backward?

The key to success in any area of your life is to focus your maximum energy on those tasks, people and activities that take you closer to your goals or at least impact your life positively in a large way. Watch out for false happiness. Gossiping can feel good when you are doing it but just like junk food, it will eventually leave you feeling bloated and guilty.

Any activity that truly contributes to your growth and makes you a better person in some way will give a subtle but definite boost to your self-esteem. You'll come out of it feeling like a better person ready to face whatever life might bring.

After you have analyzed the stats from your life, I want you to eliminate, or at least, reduce the time you spend on energy-draining activities. Follow your heart to understand what this means for you. In general, anything that negatively affects your state of mind and leaves you feeling emotionally disturbed can be an energy-draining activity.

On the other hand, I'd urge you to increase the amount of time you spend on doing things that make you feel good and that positively boost your self-esteem.

At first, this might alienate a few people or even make them angry as you'd be refusing to spend time with them doing the activities that don't add any value to your life. You have to become comfortable with making others uncomfortable, especially when this serves your highest good.

Remember, you are not helping anyone by giving them company doing wasteful activities. By saying no, you are actually doing them a favor even though they might not have the ability to recognize it at this point of time in life.

You must prioritize your own mental and emotional health over being on good terms with everyone around you. You can't please everyone. That's just the way life is.

If you try to please everyone and be a 'good' person all the time, then you are only going to accumulate frustration for yourself.

You have to also focus your energy where it will help you gain maximum results and growth. Don't allow yourself to be all over the place.

This might mean delegating the tasks that you can have others do for you. Most women find this very difficult to do. They want to do everything themselves and believe that no one can do it exactly the way they want it done. I would suggest that you let go of control a little and allow others to do some things for you. Is your perfectionism really worth the stress and pain it brings you? Is it really worth having a clean kitchen with everything exactly where you want it to be if you feel exhausted cleaning it?

Hence, ASK FOR HELP when you need it! We women expect our partners and family members to be mind readers so that they'd know exactly what we want and do it without us having to ask them to do so. If you want something, then just ask for it. This will make life less stressful for you and for everyone else.

When you have inhibitions about asking for help, just think about the worst thing that can happen if you ask for it. You might get turned down – that's not so bad. Anyway, you were going to do everything yourself. But if you do receive the help that you want (which you most likely will), then there's nothing better than that.

Don't be afraid to show the other person how you'd like them to do the task for you. However, avoid being too patronizing. Allow them to do the best that they can do and accept their help graciously. Sometimes we think that our way of doing things is the best way but remember, even that is only a perspective. Our experience of life becomes richer when we learn to see and experience things from many different perspectives.

This principle of delegation applies to all tasks – whether at home, at work, or in a social scenario. If you can ask for help and get the work done, then just ask for it. If you can pay someone to do something and save the time you'd have spent doing that task, then use the time to do more productive work (the 20% work that will bring you 80% results life).

Maybe, you could use your new-found free time to invest in a hobby class you had long wanted to attend or maybe you can add an exercise routine to your schedule. The point is to try and invest as much time as possible in doing those tasks that have the ability to transform your life and take you closer to being the person that you truly want to be.

Another important thing is to spend time with those people who make you feel uplifted while creating a little distance from those who negatively influence you. This might not be doable all the time as a lot of times the most toxic person in our life is a family member or someone we share our physical space with.

In such a situation, make sure that you are regularly taking time out to be away from this person in order to recharge your batteries. It is also important that you build emotional resilience and set clear boundaries so that this person loses his or her power to have that negative influence over you.

For instance, if this person is constantly complaining and talking negative about others, then you can refuse to participate in it. Tell them clearly that you do not want to participate in such discussions as it brings down your own energy. If they refuse to abide by your wishes, then it is alright to walk out of the room for the time being.

Just remember that no matter who that person is, you don't have to allow them to pull you down in any way. While it's crucial to have unconditional love and compassion for this person, you must not allow him or her to violate your space in any way. See the good in others no matter how badly they are behaving. You can be firm and say 'no' on the outside while having compassion for that person on the inside. As someone wisely said, "hate the sin, not the sinner." Therefore, be loving but also very firm while preserving your boundaries.

It is also a great idea to spend time with someone whose company you really enjoy. You can also enjoy alone time reading a good book, watching movies that uplift you or doing just about anything that helps you feel recharged.

Tasks for This Week:

➤ Track your time to see where you are spending it. The more focused you are on tracking every minute of your day, the clearer it will become to you where your life is going – whether you are doing the things that you really want to do or not. It will also bring you clarity as to how you can clear up your schedule to focus more on those tasks that bring you maximum returns in terms of personal satisfaction and successful results.

➤ Try to delegate at least one task that you can have someone else do for you.

➤ Ask for help when you need it and are in a position to ask someone to help.

➤ Try your best to stay away from energy-draining activities and people. Spend more time doing those things that help you feel recharged.

Week 7 – Say YES to Life!

We all have these things that we keep putting off for 'some day.' Some day we'd wear our favorite dress, join the ballet class, learn piano, take out that fine China for dinner and what not. Yet the only time we have is this present moment.

A lot of people reach the end of their earthly life feeling like they never got a chance to be truly alive. There is nothing worse than regret. Tomorrow you will regret everything you didn't do today. Also, when you constantly put off living until tomorrow, you never end up fully appreciating all the gifts that you have today.

In order to completely embrace life and make the most of it in the here and now, you must show up at your best. Wear your best clothes, use your fine china for meals, do what you really want to do on a daily basis as if today was the last day of your life (because one day you are going to be right about it). When death comes, most people don't regret the mistakes they made as much as they regret the time that they lost which they could have spent in being truly alive.

This week I want you to say 'YES' to those things that you have been putting off for later. No one knows how long they are going to live, then why not make the most of the here and now by doing exactly what you want to do.

I would also highly recommend that you start wearing your best clothes on a daily basis. Make an effort to look good. Put your best foot and face forward even if no one other than you yourself is going to be looking at you.

There is something tremendously empowering in making an effort to look our best. It automatically helps us feel better about ourselves and more confident. I don't mean that you have to wear your silk gown every day – just clothes you enjoy wearing and feel confident in.

Generally, how we choose to dress has a strong affect on how we choose to conduct ourselves. For instance, it is much easier to slump in your PJs than it is to do in a pencil skirt. Raise the bar for yourself – look your best, be your best, behave at your best every day because who knows this might be the only day you have for doing everything you want to do!

Don't save your china for guests – use them for your daily meals because you are special and you deserve to be treated that way. Don't have 'home' clothes and 'going out' clothes. Wear your best clothes every day. In the evening, retire into your night wear for sleeping – not just old worn out clothes but actual night wear. When you treat yourself as the most special person in your world, the whole Universe conspires to prove that you are right in believing so.

Tasks for This Week:

➤ Make a list of all the things that you have been putting off doing – things that really matter to you and doing them will make you feel good. Make sure that you do at least one of them this week.

➤ Wear the clothes that you truly like and enjoy every day of this whole week. Do this even if no one other than you yourself will be seeing you. In the end, the only person whose opinion of you truly matters is your own. Don't forget that when you start loving and admiring yourself, others start doing the same because, in one way or another, our relationships with others is only a reflection of our relationship with our own self. Wearing the clothes that you really like and feel confident in is a way of saying that you matter. You deserve to look your best not for anyone else but for your own self.

➤ This week, use your favorite crockery for meals even if you'd be eating all your meals alone. By living life exactly the way you want to, you send a powerful message to the Universe that you are grateful for all the blessings that have come to you so far. At the same time, you are ready for many more amazing experiences to come your way.

Week 8 – Learning to Say NO

Just like saying 'Yes' to life is important, saying 'NO' at the right time and place is equally important. A lot of times we say 'yes' to the wrong things for the wrong reasons. Usually, this happens when we don't want to disappoint the other person. We make a compromise with our own wishes and say yes to something that doesn't feel good to our heart.

The problem with this is that even though you end up looking good to the other person, you are letting your own self down. You are bound to feel resentful and also angry (most likely) towards yourself and towards that person.

It's very important to know who you are as a person, what your values are, what you are okay with, and what you are not okay with. This will help you set powerful boundaries. Not having boundaries will constantly make you feel as if you are being pushed in different directions by other people. Taking a firm stand for yourself is necessary for living a happy and fulfilling life.

This week, I want to ask you to get in touch with your heart more deeply than ever. Every time someone asks you for something, don't just jump onto answer it. Take a few moments and gauge how you feel inside your heart. Say yes, only if you truly want to say so. Saying NO gently but firmly is an art. It is surely one of the most important skills one can have.

We usually take life for granted. We think we have forever to live so we spend a lot of time doing those things that we don't really want to do but feel obliged to do. I am challenging you to understand and fully appreciate the fact that every day of life is a gift – one that can be taken away from you any moment any day.

If this day was your last, would you still say 'Yes' to whatever it is you are considering doing at this moment? If the answer is 'NO' then just say No and walk away. You might not be able to make everyone happy but that's alright. It's not your responsibility to make everyone happy. The only person whose happiness is solely and completely your responsibility is you yourself.

People are bound to get upset when you don't give them what they want from you but that's alright too. You have to get comfortable with the fact that sometimes in the process of ensuring your own happiness and doing what's best for you, you will unwittingly upset other people. How they deal with it is up to them.

You are not obligated to do their bidding. This is not selfish or egoistic. Sometimes saying no is the most loving thing to do as by doing that you are honoring your soul while offering your Truth to the other person. As a thumb rule, never say yes to someone if that will leave you burning with rage and resentment inside.

Now, there might be some situations where saying NO is just not possible or at least the consequences of saying NO will be so severe that you won't be able to handle the repercussions.

I would say that there is a way around everything. You can at least express to the other person that you don't really want to say yes but are feeling obligated to do so. This might help you both in reaching a compromise.

If even this does not seem doable, and you feel like there is no way out, then I would suggest trying to see what you can learn from this experience. Try to see it as something that is going to help you become a better person. It might seem impossible to glean such wisdom from it at the moment but try to find the pearl hidden in the oyster.

At the end of the day, just remember that it is not worth doing anything with resentment and anger in your heart. Therefore, I will still say that sticking with your own Truth is always the best choice. Say NO to anything that your heart doesn't agree with.

Eventually, you have to become comfortable with people not liking it when you say NO, especially when you know in your heart that you are doing the right thing. You can't please everyone, and that's alright. Everyone is responsible for their own happiness. Your responsibility is your own happiness first and foremost.

Besides, you are causing more damage to your relationship with that person by saying a yes that is fraught with tension and resentment. A loving and firm NO is much better than a resentful Yes in the long-run. The more firmly you establish your boundaries, the more people will be willing to respect it. It might not happen right away but eventually this will surely be the case.

For now, I'd urge you to say NO to all those activities, food, places and people that don't serve your highest good. For instance, if getting in shape has been on your list, then saying NO to junk food and Yes to the gym should be on your agenda this week. Don't put off things for an elusive tomorrow.

Our time on this earth is finite and limited at best. Learn to act in the here and now! You want to gain every experience that your heart craves and end every day with the satisfaction that you lived the day as best as you could while making the most of every opportunity that came your way.

Therefore, say NO to procrastination. Say NO to all your bad habits. Make small changes today and act on them because the journey of a thousand miles always begins with a small step in the right direction.

If you feel confused, then listen more attentively to your intuition – your heart has all the answers that you are seeking. You just have to quieten the din of your mind to hear the voice of your soul.

Let all your actions, words and thoughts be guided by your higher self. Put your heart and soul in every moment – live every day as if it were your last. You'll be amazed by the miracles you manage to create!

Task for This Week:

➤ Say NO to all the things, people and circumstances that don't resonate with your soul. It might not be easy to implement this fully but at least make a start somewhere. Say NO to at least one thing that doesn't feel right to you. Free yourself from anger and resentment. Every time you do something because you HAVE to do it, rather than because you truly want to do it, you are building resentment. Nothing is more destructive than the emotions of anger and resentment. Stay away from them as much as possible.

Week 9 – Give Love to Yourself

I have said this before and I am going to say this again: the most important relationship in the world is the relationship you have with yourself. The harder you work on this one relationship, the more rewarding life will become and the better your relationships with other people will be.

In order to be more loving towards yourself, I'll suggest that you incorporate rituals into your daily life. The right kind of self-care rituals will help you deepen your relationship with your body, mind and soul.

One of the most powerful ways of connecting with your body is by doing a daily self-massage. In Ayurveda, the ancient system of healing from

India, this is known as 'abhyanga.' What's interesting is that the Sanskrit word for oil is 'sneha.' 'Sneha' also means affection. Hence, the act of performing abhyanga or body massage (with oil) is an act of giving love to oneself.

There is something tremendously healing in the power of touch. When you touch yourself with love and care, you deliver a positive message to your mind – one that reinforces the fact that you and your needs are important. If you do a daily self-massage, then you also become very sensitive to the needs of your body and all the changes that are happening in it constantly. For instance, you will be able to identify the smallest of changes that start taking place in your body before your menstrual period begins to set in. You also learn how to take better care of yourself based on all the signs that your body is providing you.

Doing a self-massage is one of the daily prescriptions given in Ayurveda for maintaining optimal health. It not only relaxes and rejuvenates the body but also puts the mind at ease.

Another practice that I would highly recommend is journaling. There is nothing more powerful than writing down your thoughts, emotions, feelings and observations on a day-to-day basis. Jim Rohn famously said, "A life worth living is a life worth recording."

No matter what you are going through – how good or challenging your day has been – writing things down will help you put things into perspective. You will be able to develop a deeper understanding of the circumstances that you are currently being presented with. This understanding will help you in coming up with solutions. Looking back at old diary records will also help you remember all the wonderful times you have enjoyed.

I would also highly recommend that you write down three things that you are grateful for at the end of every day. Sometimes you might think you have nothing to be grateful for but that's just not true. We take a lot of things for granted. You could be grateful for the fact that you have a bed to sleep on, a diary to write in, a pen to write with. There are so many people who don't even have these basic things and would consider themselves enormously privileged to have your life despite all its challenges.

Gratitude is also the most powerful form of prayer. By saying thanks you are making room for the Universe to send you more things to be grateful for. Blessings attract more blessings in life. If you will focus your energy on complaining, then you will manifest more of what you dislike.

Be grateful for every experience as it is here to help you learn an important lesson. In fact, if you want to transform the situations of your life, then you must first be grateful for every experience that you have been presented with. Even if you can't see the silver lining it, trust that it exists. The more negative energy you project onto something, the greater the problem becomes. Thinking of something as a problem is in itself an act of magnifying the negativity contained in it.

You must change your mindset because unless you increase your vibrational frequency with gratitude and love, you will keep on attracting challenging situations in life. The people and outer circumstances might change but the root of the issue will remain the same because every challenge has come in your life to teach you something. The only way you can release it completely is by fully embracing the seed of wisdom that is present in it.

Tasks for This Week:

➤ Start doing a daily full-body massage. Ayurveda recommends using medicated cold-pressed sesame oil for this. The best time to do this massage is in the morning. It would be ideal if you could make this a daily routine but even if you aren't able to do that, at least aim to do one or two full body massages every week.

➤ Start your day and end your day with gratitude. Every morning before getting out of bed, say a small prayer of gratitude in your mind or out aloud. Count at least 3 things you are grateful for. Every time you encounter a challenge in your day, remind yourself that you must be grateful for the lesson that is brought to you through it. Fully embrace the lesson – allow your heart to pulsate with unconditional love and gratitude towards it. This way, you can transform any circumstance of life.

➤ Get in the habit of daily journaling. At night, write down at least three things you are grateful for. Some days it might be hard to do this practice but remember that those are the days you need to do this practice even more. When you develop the habit of finding the pearls of wisdom hidden inside every situation of life, you build the ability to face any circumstance of life with tenacity and strength. Also, don't forget that the only way you can attract more blessings in your life is by being grateful for the blessings that you already have in your life.

Love is the most powerful healer. Gratitude is the most powerful magnet that will attract more good things into your life. By performing the physical act of writing down what you are grateful for, you are hardwiring the brain to see the best in every situation. Hence, I encourage you to not just mentally or verbally speak what you are grateful for but also foster the habit of writing things down. This way you are truly internalizing these positive habits. Every day reflect on your day to find the silver lining in everything.

Week 10 – Connect with the Natural World

Nature is the most powerful healer. The further away we move from nature, the more diseased our society becomes. Being healthy is very simple – we just need to abide by the laws of nature and live a life that's in sync with natural laws.

The most important thing I'd suggest you do this week is build a stronger relationship with the rhythms of nature. Go to bed early and wake up early. If possible, try to go to bed by 9 or 10 and wake up as early as possible (ideally, not any later than 6). This might involve making a huge change to your current routine. I would suggest that you take your time with this (you don't have to get to the ideal routine in just one week).

To begin with, start by going to bed 15 minutes earlier than your usual time and get out of bed 15 minutes early. Continue changing your sleep schedule every week by 15 minutes until you reach the ideal.

You will be amazed by the health benefits you derive from this simple practice. Most people think that the duration of sleep is the most important thing. This is not the true. What matters most is the quality of sleep one gets.

Inside our body there is a clock that is meant to be in sync with nature. It's called the circadian rhythm. The body is meant to be rested and rejuvenated at night through the process of sleep. Daytime is meant for activity.

To bring your circadian rhythm in a state of balance, follow the cycle of day and night. Wake up before sunrise, have the largest meal of the day when the sun is at its peak. The reason why noon is the best time to have a heavy meal is because the energy of the sun aids the body to digest a heavy meal. If you ate the same food at 8 pm, it will take your body much longer to digest the same meal and it would also require the body to expend greater energy in the process.

Try to cut off all stimulating activities and exposure to digital devices 3-4 hours before sleep.

If that's too difficult, then enforce a digital ban at least an hour before bed.

Take the time to go for a relaxing walk, gaze at the stars, journal, or do anything else that will help you release the stresses of the day. Also, make sure that you have a very light dinner at least 3-4 hours before bedtime. Go to bed on an empty or relatively light stomach as much as possible. This is will give your body a break from digestion – allowing it to focus on detoxification and rejuvenation.

I want you to understand that it's not enough to just eat healthy or sleep a certain number of hours. You must do them at the right time every day. You have to also retain consistency as much as possible by doing all activities at the same time every day (even on weekends). You only have to be more attentive to realize that sleeping in the daytime can never be a replacement for night sleep. Similarly, sleeping from 1 am to 8 pm can never give you the same benefits as sound sleep that is enjoyed between 10 pm to 5 or 6 am.

By doing all this, your energy levels will go up. You'll enjoy excellent health and feel rejuvenated.

I would highly encourage you to create a positive routine for yourself that is in sync with the cycle of day and night. If, for some reason, this is impossible for you – like you have a job that demands you to stay awake all night or there are obligations that make it impossible for you to follow a good sleep schedule or have your meals on time – I would suggest that you incorporate some other positive health practices in your routine.

For instance, keep your room as dark as possible so that you can trick your body into relaxing more and having deep sleep even during the day. Also, try to have the largest meal of the day at noon or at least by 1.30 pm. Have an early dinner by 7 pm and if you feel the need to snack at night time, try to eat something light like fruits and salads.

If it's possible, then, eventually, you'd want to consider making a shift to a job that allows you to maintain a normal schedule. Going against nature's biological clock does take a very heavy toll on the body. If a change of job is something you can't create, then make the most of what you can do by incorporating as healthy a routine as possible. Also, in that case, try to go to bed and wake up at the same time even on weekends. The body does not like change – all deviations from the routine disrupt the normal functioning of the organ systems.

Another extremely beneficial practice I would like you to incorporate in your day would be to go for a walk in the park every day in the morning. Walk bare feet – feel the grass, the tress, the sunshine. Listen to the chirping of birds. It's hard to explain how this therapy works but by simply being in nature and allowing yourself to experience all its glory, you immediately start feeling elated and refreshed. If you live close to a forest and can go there for a walk, then that's even better. If not, then a walk in the park would be just as beneficial.

You can also go for a walk in the evening. However, the benefits of an early morning walk don't compare with the benefits of an evening walk. To get the best of both worlds, go for both. If that's not possible, then, at least, start going for the morning walk. If you live close to a beach, then you can also go for a walk on the beach. When you start your day by connecting with nature, you feel much more energetic throughout the day.

Tasks for This Week:

➤ Ty to go to bed by 9 or 10 pm. Wake up as early as possible. Ideally, wake up before sunrise. If you can't, then try to wake up around the time of sunrise. According to Ayurveda, we should not sleep past sunrise as this makes the body sluggish and encourages laziness. If your current schedule is too far off from this ideal routine, then slowly condition your body to follow this timetable. Every week try to go to bed earlier by 15 minutes and wake up 15 minutes earlier. Keep making the change until you have fully adopted the new routine.

➤ Have breakfast by 8.30 am, lunch by 12.30 pm, and dinner by 6 pm. You can make small variations in the timings but try to stick to this timeline as much as possible.

➤ Go for a walk in nature every morning after waking up. Walk bare feet on the grass, watch the rising sun, listen to the chirping of birds, feel the fresh morning air on your skin, soak the sunshine on your face – you will be amazed by how this practice transforms your body, mind and soul. You can also go for an evening stroll in addition to the morning walk. If a morning walk is not possible for you, then you can go only for the evening stroll (although a morning walk would be much more beneficial). Try to spend at least 5-10 minutes every day (if you can manage more, then that's even better) in nature.

➤ Take the time to gaze at the stars as often as possible. There is something absolutely magical about star gazing. When we are looking at the magnificent night sky, suddenly, all our problems and suffering start feeling very small in comparison to the infinite vistas our eyes are beholding in that moment.

It's fine even if it takes you a long time to incorporate all these suggestions into your daily routine. Make a start somewhere this week and allow yourself to make small changes and improvements every couple of days. It might take you a few weeks or even months to fully incorporate this routine but don't give up on it. I promise you that it will all be worthwhile in the end.

Week 11 – Appreciate Beauty

Beauty has the power to heal the soul. When you have the ability to see and appreciate the beauty that surrounds you every moment, you are also able to transform the ordinary into the exquisite. This week, I want you to develop an eye for beauty. It will make your life a lot more joyful. Life will no longer be ordinary. Instead, it will become a grand celebration of the infinity of existence.

Beauty touches and arouses something very deep in us. It awakens us to the inherent immortality of the spirit that is encased within the limits of this body.

Piero Ferrucci, in his book, *Beauty and the Soul,* discusses the power of beauty to heal the soul. Just imagine how different your life will be if, while walking down the sidewalk instead of thinking about how many stresses you have in your life, you took a moment to admire the blue sky that lies above your eyes. If, instead of hurriedly eating your lunch at your work desk, you took a moment to relish the delicious flavors of a home cooked meal that was prepared with love.

A lot of times people think that beauty is something that is experienced on occasion through something big like a beautiful wedding, a lakeside resort, a carefully decorated house. Yet the truth is that beauty is everywhere – it is currently surrounding you and smiling at you through a million forms. You just have to open your eyes to appreciate how miraculous our existence really is.

Some people think that beauty is something frivolous and serves no real purpose. It's true that there might not be a purpose behind the beauty of a blooming flower, the compositions of Mozart, the poetry of William Wordsworth, the musical compositions of Beethoven. But can you imagine what the world will be like without these?

Beauty is something that affects us at the level of the soul. It alters our emotional state – it has the power to arouse emotions so deep that the mind can never comprehend them. It's not something that can be understood with logic. It must be felt, experienced, and expressed with the heart.

When you begin to seek and find beauty in everyday life, something inside you shifts. Suddenly, your experience of life becomes richer and much more immersive. Your inner world becomes imbued with a fragrance so surreal that everything around you feels magical.

When you are experiencing something beautiful, you forget all your worries. You get a chance to glimpse at eternity. Your heart experiences a fulfillment so pure that nothing matters in that moment – simply being alive is enough. Those are moments when we truly understand why we are here – it's not an intellectual understanding but simply an experience of infinity where to just 'be' is enough.

Think of the most beautiful moments of your life – you'll perhaps think of a hug given by a loved one, the unforgettable laughter of a baby, the fragrance of a rose, the moment you got engaged, a lovely sunset that you watched with your lover, holding the hand of someone you love immensely. You might also be reflecting on moments when you were looking your best and everyone showered you with compliments. Having an appreciation for beauty doesn't mean appreciating only that which is outside of you but also your own inner and outer beauty.

This week I want to urge you to appreciate your own beauty and the beauty surrounding you. Every day find something beautiful and write down a few lines inspired by it in your journal. You can do this in addition with your gratitude practice. It doesn't have to be anything lengthy. Even just one or two lines are enough. If you feel like it, then you are certainly welcome to write more. You must feel what you are writing – allow your heart to soak the emotions that you are seeking to express through words.

Also, regularly do something that makes you feel beautiful. This could mean wearing your favorite clothes more often or taking time off for a pampering spa day. Understand that you deserve to feel beautiful, adored, admired and loved. You must be your own greatest lover – the more deeply you fall in love with yourself, the richer your experiences with a romantic partner will become.

Every other relationship is only a reflection of your relationship with yourself. If you love and accept yourself unconditionally, then you will also be able to experience this with a partner. The world outside is only a reflection of the world inside. You must feel beautiful in order to look your best.

Tasks for This Week:

➤ Find beauty in everyday life and journal about it. It could be something as small as how stunning halved cherry tomatoes look on a wooded chopping board or a flight of birds you got to witness on your walk back home after work, a beautiful face you saw on the bus, a delicately crafted chandelier you found at the antique shop, the perfect symmetry of a leaf you held up against the morning sun. Anything can become a source of inspiration if you are willing to become a poet of beauty.

➤ Do something to feel beautiful every day. It could mean taking an elaborate bath every morning and/or wearing your best clothes every day. I have noticed that a lot of women put off wearing their best clothes or using their best things for some special day which is yet to come. I am urging you to make every day special by looking, feeling, doing and being your best. Just remember that any day can be your last – there is nothing worse than a life of regrets. Therefore, live every day as if it were your last because one day you are going to be right.

Week 12 – Practice Love and Kindness Towards All Creatures

What you give is what you receive back manyfold. Love and kindness are the balms that soothe the soul. By being kind and loving towards others, you allow your own heart to heal. Nothing is more powerful for healing the soul than the practice of giving love. However, you must never give from a place of expectation. Even the desire for recognition or appreciation takes away the unconditionality from love. Every kind word, every loving gesture, comes back to us multiplied. The same holds true for unkindness and hatred.

The greatest art in life is to practice giving without any expectations. There shouldn't even be any desire for recognition or appreciation. A lot of times people complain that because of how 'giving' they are, others take advantage of them. To this, my simple reply is that you haven't mastered the art of giving unconditionally yet.

A simple rule of thumb I have for myself when I am about to do something for someone is that I ask myself, "Will I do this even if I wasn't going to receive anything in return for it – not even appreciation? Will I do this without feeling the need to tell anyone else about this?" I know it's the right thing for me to do only when the answer is YES to all these questions.

You have to tap into that state of perfect unconditional giving when you decide to do anything for anyone. Even a small desire for appreciation can taint the purity of this desire. It's better to not do something if you aren't doing it from a place of unconditional giving.

Also, learn to expand the circle of your love and kindness to include all creatures. We are born in a family so that we may learn to love one another unconditionally but love for family is only the starting point on this expansive journey of all-inclusive love. To completely master the art of loving without conditions, you have to feel love for everyone including towards those whom you believe to be your enemies or someone who has harmed you in any way.

When your love becomes all-inclusive, at that point, you will realize that you find friends and well-wishers everywhere. When you start extending a helping hand to your near and dear ones and also to perfect strangers, you will realize that so many people come forward to help you in times of need. When you help others get what they want, the Universe makes it easy for you to get what you want.

Tasks for This Week:

➤ This week do something for someone without expecting anything in return. You don't need to do something big. It can be something small like feeding the birds, giving a sincere compliment to a stranger, or helping a friend cook dinner. The only criteria is that you must be able to do this without any desire for recognition or appreciation. Notice how this act makes you feel. Write down in your journal all the positive emotions you get to experience.

➤ Feel grateful for the big and small things other people do for you. Perhaps your partner left you a loving note in the car, a stranger stopped by to help you fix your car, a baby came running to you in the park and gave you a hug for no reason. A lot of times we take others for granted. Be grateful for all the big and small surprises life brings to you. Take the time to say a heartfelt 'Thank You' to everyone who does something nice for you.

➤ Never go to bed in anger. Let go of all grudges and memories of wrongdoings. Your health, peace and happiness are too precious to be sacrificed at the altar of such memories. Forgive others easily and promptly not because they need it but because you don't want be a prisoner of your own anger and hatred. Understand that everyone is doing the best they can based on the knowledge and understanding they have. You don't need to tell them verbally that you are forgiving them – forgiveness has to be mental and emotional – it must come from the soul as only then it can reach another soul. Life is too short to form negative entanglements with any soul. If you have done anything wrong, then seek forgiveness immediately. Tell them you are sorry. Never let ego get in the way as the ego's way is the path of inordinate suffering. You want to be free from all negative bonds as your own wellbeing is far more precious than anything else.

Bonus Chapter – Two Important Life Hacks That You Must Master

Understanding and gaining a certain level of mastery over these two life hacks has really changed my life. I want to share this wisdom with you so that you can also implement it and experience great transformation.

Life Hack #1 – Understanding The Difference Between Pain and Suffering

We all go through dark times. Hardships force us to become a better version of ourselves. Of course, some people just choose to wail in misery dwelling perpetually in a self-created hell.

You must understand that pain is unavoidable but suffering is always a choice. While most people view pain as an enemy, it is really our friend. Pain is there to tell us when we are going in the wrong direction. Some children are born with a congenital insensitivity to pain. This prevents them from having any physical experience of pain.

Due to the absence of pain, their childhood is especially difficult. They get injured more frequently since they have no perception of pain. Can you even imagine how nightmarish this must be as you could lose or severely damage a body part without even knowing what has happened. It is pain that makes you instantly pull your finger out of an electric socket. Without pain you wouldn't be able to protect your physical body from all the damaging forces and threats that are present in the environment.

Pain is the compass that guides you to the right path every time you mistakenly start moving in the wrong direction. Don't be afraid of pain – make it your ally. Once you embrace your pain, it will stop hurting you so much.

Embracing your pain does not mean that you have to become miserable because of what is going on with you. To embrace your pain means listening to what your body and mind are telling you. To acknowledge your pain means realizing that you were going in the wrong direction and now is the time to change your path.

Suffering is Always a Choice

Let's say that your friend Jenna said something nasty about you. When you heard her unkind words, you felt pain in your heart. You acknowledged this pain by accepting that her words have indeed caused some wounds to you. However, next moment, you realized that whatever she said is her opinion of you.

After all, people don't see others as who they really. They only see a reflection of themselves in others. When you thought about this, it made no sense to hold onto Jenna's opinion of you. You let the incident go with understanding and compassion as you understood that no one will say such unkind things about another person unless they are themselves suffering in some way. Unkindness can come only from someone who is struggling to love and accept their own self unconditionally. This would then be a perfect example of feeling the pain but choosing to not suffer.

Now let's look at the second scenario. You heard Jenna's words and it really hurt you. Instead of acknowledging your pain and letting it go the next moment. You chose to replay in your mind what she has said to you. You told others just how unkind Jenna is and narrated everything she said about you. You mentally and verbally kept repeating her hurtful words. This is what I mean when I say you have turned your pain into a suffering. When you dwell on the pain you felt at a particular moment, you bring that pain into your present, and make yourself truly miserable.

People can suffer for weeks, months, years or even an entire life because of the pain they received in a few moments of life. I would tell you to guard against this tendency. The only person you are punishing with this kind of suffering is your own self. The cost of holding onto suffering is too high. You are trading your health and your wellbeing by holding onto a negative memory.

The same thing applies for physical pain. You could have a severe bout of cold but that does not mean you have to *suffer* from the cold. While the physical discomfort of having the cold will certainly make you uncomfortable, you can turn this into a living hell by dwelling on the pain. If you start thinking too much about how miserable you are because of the cold, then you'll easily turn your pain into a grand suffering. If you embrace the pain, then you will allow the healing process to happen much quicker and without excessive suffering.

Feel the pain but protect yourself from suffering. Never allow the past to ruin your present. Even what happened earlier today is history, it doesn't exist. It exists only in your mind. You have the power to not let it claim your happiness and sanity in the present moment.

Coming Out of Old Suffering

No matter where you are in life right now, you have the power to change – the ability to create a positive future and a beautiful now.

The way to loosen your grip over old suffering is by becoming grateful for everything you have right now. Every time you find yourself dwelling on past wrongdoings and painful memories, take a pen and make a list of everything that you are grateful for right now.

Life Hack #2 – How to Relate with Others

Something that happens with every person who starts a journey of self-transformation is that they start trying to change other people in their lives. It is only natural for that person to wonder why everyone else is writhing in a quagmire of self-pity when there is so much beauty and joy around them right at this very moment.

It's very difficult to resist the urge to tell others how they aren't ever going to go anywhere with their pessimistic attitude. Yet offering any form of unsolicited advice is likely to backfire.

The question is how should we relate to others when their choices are very different from our own and we don't agree with their way of life?

Undertaking a spiritual journey is the most exciting thing any person can ever do. We feel such incomprehensible delight that we want to share our discoveries with others. While this idea in itself is quite a noble one, we must understand that every person born in this school of human life has a unique curriculum.

Everyone is here to learn something. You can't hasten the process for them. In reality, grief is the greatest teacher, loss is the biggest redeemer, pain is our most faithful friend as it tells us when we are going in the wrong direction. Suffering comes only when we choose to ignore that little voice which is constantly whispering to us in our hearts and has the answer to all our questions.

Give up on your attachments – nothing belongs to you, no one belongs with you. Even the idea of this 'I' is not going to last forever. Would you go and lecture a woman on the street how she must live her life in order to experience the joy and delight you are currently experiencing? Most likely you wouldn't entertain such an idea.

Why do you constantly want to tell your loved ones that they must change? Give up on your attachments. Stop clinging onto to the idea of 'I' and mine. Be of service to others and help them when they ask for it but don't expect them to be anything like you just because you happen to call them mother, father, brother, sister, husband, wife or as any other relation.

Understand that you are here for your own purpose. The journey within must be taken alone and that's the beauty of it.

One of my most favorite things to do is to sit on a beach and watch the waves crashing by the shore. I love the sound of crashing waves – there is something supremely primal about that moment as if it revokes an ancient memory. A memory of where I come from – a memory of where we all come from. A memory that reminds me there is nowhere to go, nothing to achieve – just this moment to experience without attachments.

When someone is saying something good to you or bad to you, learn to witness it the way you would witness the waves of the ocean. You wouldn't go out there and tell a wave to not rise so high or so low – you'll just watch it. Give up your attachment with the idea of right or wrong, good or bad, positive or negative.

The whole world is only a play of consciousness. Everyone is an actor playing his or her part perfectly. Would you jump on the stage to tell an actor not to be so morose when he is playing the role of a sad and dejected person? You wouldn't, you'd witness it. You'd jump on the stage to help the actor if it was requested. Otherwise, you will just hold onto your seat and watch the drama of human life unfold before you.

You must understand that people change only when they want to change. The only thing you can ever do for others is to be an inspiration – a positive role model they can look up to. Let them be who they are because they have each chosen a role that befits what they want to learn during this brief play of human life.

Every time your mind drifts away into memories of the past or in anticipation of the future, bring it back to the present by focusing on your breath.

All your struggles will cease when you'll stop trying to make life happen to you or for you. Instead, just let it happen through you. Do what you have to do – but let it be without any attachments and expectations.

Suffering comes only when we lack the ability to witness all that is there in this moment. Suffering comes when we are caught up in the memories of the past or attached to the outcomes of the future. Suffering begins from that moment when we start trying to become something just to make us believe that we are the 'I' that we think we are. Trying to hold on to this illusory 'I' is like trying to capture sand in a fist. The 'I' is the rainbow you can never catch and yet the illusion of it makes you dig countless trenches to get to it.

That doesn't mean you should become passive and not take any action. The point is to act the way you'd act if you were playing a role in a movie. You'll do your best while remaining conscious of the fact that you are only playing a character. To do what you know in your heart you are here to do, without any attachments to the outcome it will bring you, is the real purpose of life.

Be constantly active but never reactive. Play your part in the movie of life to perfection but never forget that you aren't the 'I' that you believe you are.

I Need Your Help...

I want to thank you for taking this 12-week journey with me. I hope that I have been able to help you with transforming your life and your relationship with yourself.

Even though this book has come to an end, please understand that this is only the beginning of a new life for you. I want to urge you to continue the self-love and self-care practices you have adopted through this book.

No matter what you are going through in life, please never forget that you can't pour from an empty cup. Prioritize your needs above everything else because you can give to others when you have more than enough for yourself.

If this book has proven helpful to you in any way, then I'd like to ask you for a favor. Would you be kind enough to write a review for this book on Amazon?

It's my dream to help as many people as possible through my work. Your testimony might inspire someone else to pick this book and change their life. So please, do leave a review.